HELP IS ON THE WAY FOR:

Maps & Globes

Written by Marilyn Berry
Pictures by Bartholomew

CHILDRENS PRESS ™

CHICAGO

Childrens Press
School and Library Edition

Executive Producer: Marilyn Berry
Editor: Theresa Tinkle
Consultants: Patricia Harrington and Terie Snyder
Design: Abigail Johnston
Typesetting: Curt Chelin

ISBN 0-516-03242-9

So you need to learn about **maps and globes.**

Hang on! Help is on the way!

If you are having a hard time

- finding places on a map,
- understanding the parts of a map,
- using an atlas or a gazetteer. . .

. . .you are not alone!

Just in case you're wondering...

...why don't we start at the beginning?

What Are Maps and Globes?

Maps are drawings or pictures of the earth. Some include the entire surface of the earth. Others show only a small section of the earth's surface. There are also maps and globes of outer space and of imaginary places.

Why Are Maps and Globes Important?

Maps and globes offer a wealth of information in a simple, easy-to-read form. There will be many occasions when you will find maps and globes useful. Here are some examples:

- Giving directions

- Planning trips

- Understanding current events

Looking for information on a map or globe is like going on a treasure hunt. Finding the information can be fun and easy when you learn how to use all the clues. The key is to take it one step at a time.

Globes

A globe is a map that is shaped like a ball. It is the only type of map that can show you the whole earth's surface in its true shape. A globe is a good type of map to use when you want to
- look at a map of the whole world in its real form,
- see where one place is in relation to the rest of the world, or
- see how the earth is tilted and how it rotates.

Locating Places on the Globe

A globe is divided into sections by imaginary lines.

- The horizontal lines that run east and west are called **parallels of latitude**.
- The vertical lines that run north and south are called **meridians of longitude**.
- When all the lines are drawn, they form the **global grid**. This grid makes it possible for us to transfer information from a globe onto a flat map. It also makes it possible for us to locate points on a globe and measure the distance between them.

The Parallels of Latitude

The parallels of latitude are horizontal lines used to measure distance north and south. They are called "parallels" because they are always the same distance apart. There are five major parallels of latitude.

- **The Equator** circles the earth at its widest point, and divides it into the northern and southern hemispheres.
- **The Tropic of Cancer** and the **Arctic Circle** are between the Equator and the North Pole.
- **The Tropic of Capricorn** and the **Antarctic Circle** are between the Equator and the South Pole.

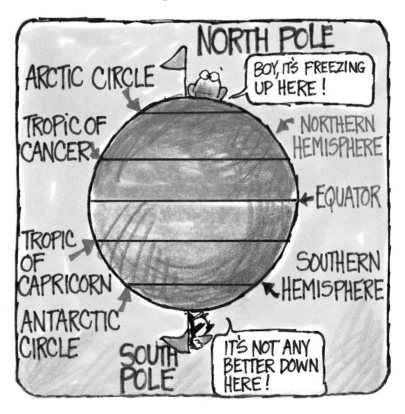

Parallels of latitude are numbered in units called *degrees.* the number of degrees tells how far each line is from the Equator. Here is how the numbering system works:

- The Equator is the center of the earth, so it is labelled 0 degrees.
- The North Pole is 90 degrees north of the Equator.
- The South Pole is 90 degrees south of the Equator.
- All other parallels of latitude fall in between.

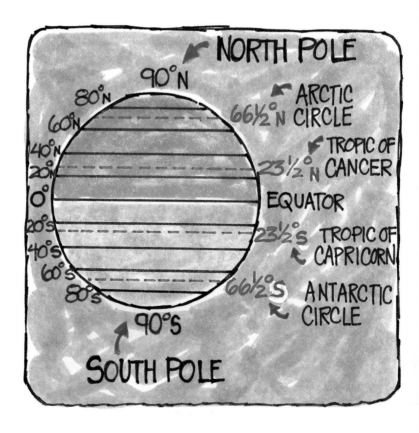

The Meridians of Longitude

The meridians of longitude are vertical lines that are used to measure distance east and west. They are not parallel as are the latitude lines. As the meridians of longitude approach the Poles, they fall closer together. There are two major meridians of longitude.

- **The Prime Meridian** runs from the North Pole through Greenwich, England and then to the South Pole. It divides the earth into the eastern hemisphere and the western hemisphere.
- **The International Date Line** runs from the North Pole through the Pacific Ocean and then to the South Pole. It falls on the opposite side of the earth from the Prime Meridian.

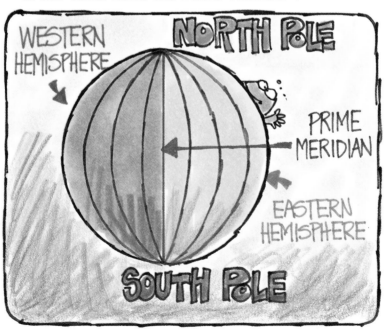

Meridians of longitude lines are also numbered in degrees. However, the number of degrees on meridians of longitude tells how far each line is from the Prime Meridian. Here is how the numbering system works:

- The Prime Meridian is the starting point, so it is labelled 0 degrees.
- The International Date Line is exactly halfway around the earth, so it is labelled 180 degrees.
- All other meridians of longitude fall in between on either the east side or the west side.

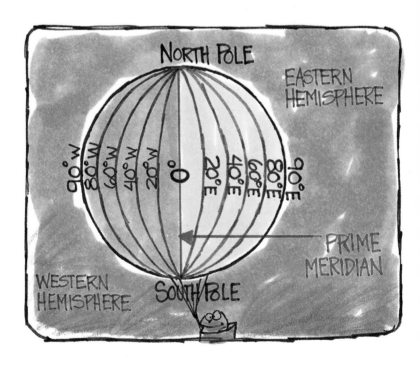

With both latitude and longitude lines drawn on the globe, you have the framework for locating any place on earth. Practice using latitude and longitude lines by finding the place where 40 degrees south and 20 degrees east cross. (Hint: The place is marked with an *.)

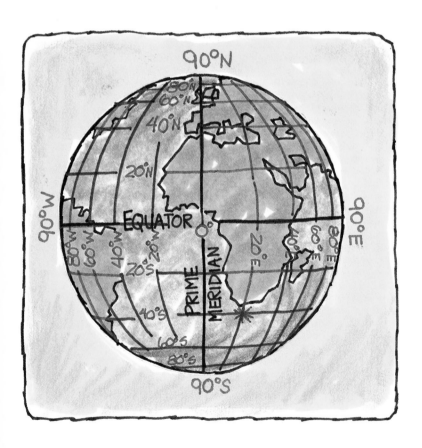

Maps

Maps do not have the bulky shape of a globe. Maps are flat and are much more convenient to carry and store. Maps also offer many other kinds of information. There are three different types of maps:

- Physical maps
- Political maps
- Special purpose maps

Physical Maps

Physical maps show the natural features of the earth's surface. They show the different forms of the land such as mountains and valleys. They also show water formations such as rivers, lakes, and streams. There are two types of physical maps: **relief maps** and **topographical maps**.

- **Relief maps** show the appearance of the earth's surface. Color and shading are used to point out the different land and water formations. Some relief maps actually have a raised surface to emphasize the texture of the earth.

- **Topographical maps** show the earth's surface by using *contour lines*. A contour line shows the height of the land. All of the land along one contour line is the same height. This type of map is not colorful, but it is a good way to show how flat or steep the land is. Here are two important tips that will help you read contour lines:

1. When the lines appear far apart, the land is flat.
2. When the lines appear close together, the land is steep.

Political Maps

Political maps offer a different type of information. They show the boundaries continents, countries, states, counties, cities, and towns. Political maps often use color to show how the land is divided. Since boundaries can change, it's a good idea to check the date on a political map to make sure you are getting current information.

Special Purpose Maps

Special purpose maps offer a variety of information. The titles will usually tell you the kind of information you will find on this type of map. Here are some examples of special purpose maps:

- weather maps
- population maps
- natural resources maps
- products maps
- time zone maps
- road maps

It is also a good idea to check the date of special purpose maps to make sure the information is current.

Locating Places on a Map

You can usually locate a place on a map by using one of two different methods.

1. **Using latitude and longitude.** Some maps are marked with a grid of latitude and longitude. The degrees of latitude are listed down the side of the map. The degrees of longitude are listed across the top or bottom of the map. If you know the latitude and longitude of a place, you can locate it on the map by finding the point where the two lines cross.

2. **Using a map index.** Some maps have an index that lists all the places that can be found on the map. The places are listed in alphabetical order, and each one is followed by a letter and a number. The letter and number are to be used as a guide for finding the place you want.

How To Use an Index

- Look in the index and find the place you want to locate on the map.
- Read the letter and number printed next to the place and write them on a piece of paper.
- Along one side of the map you will find a column of letters. Find the letter you need.
- Along the top of the map you will find a row of numbers. Find the number you need.
- Draw an imaginary line with your finger across the row. Then draw a second imaginary line down the column.
- Where the two lines cross, you will find the place you are looking for.

Map and Globe Skills

Being able to locate a place on a map or globe is an important skill. However, there are three other skills that are also important.

- Understanding directions
- Using the scale
- Using the key

Understanding Directions

There are four main directions that are used with maps. They are: north, south, east, and west. They are called **cardinal directions**. Sometimes the cardinal directions are combined to make **intermediate directions**. The intermediate directions are: northwest, northeast, southwest, and southeast.

In order to read a map correctly, you need to know how the directions are arranged. On most maps

- North is at the top,
- South is at the bottom,
- East is on the right, and
- West is on the left.

Most maps have a symbol that shows the directions. The symbol is either a *compass rose,* which shows all four directions, or an arrow that points north. This symbol is especially helpful when the top of the map points in a direction other than north. It's always a good idea to check the direction symbol, just to make sure you understand which way the map faces.

Using the Scale

It would be impossible to draw everything on a map in its actual size. Therefore, maps are miniature versions of real places. This is called "drawing to scale."

A map can be either a large-scale picture of an area or a small-scale picture of the same area.

- **Large-scale maps** cover a small section of land but show a great amount of detail.

- **Small-scale maps** cover a much larger area of land but show very little detail.

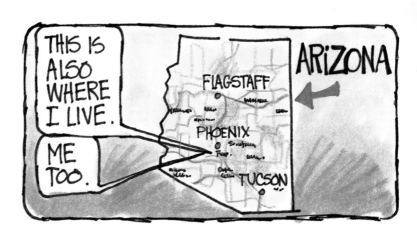

A map scale helps you measure the actual distance between two points on a map. The scale can be stated in three different ways. For example:

- In words: 1 inch represents 100 miles.
- As a ratio: 1: 100 or 1/100.
- As a sample: ⌊_____⌋
  100 miles

LET'S SEE... ONE INCH EQUALS 100 MILES AND IT'S THREE AND A HALF INCHES... THAT MAKES IT 350 MILES TO THE BORDER.

HMMM

FROGS DON'T HAVE SCALES.

There are two ways to measure distance
on a map.

- **Direct distance** is the shortest distance between
  two points. It is easily measured with a ruler.
- **Road distance** is always greater than direct
  distance. It is also more difficult to measure
  because the roads do not follow a straight line.

Using the Key

A map key (sometimes called a legend) explains how the information is displayed on a map. It is usually located in one of the lower corners of the map. Maps use many different symbols for displaying information. To get the most out of a map, you will need to look at the key and become familiar with its symbols.

Picture symbols are used a lot on special purpose maps for showing information such as:

- Road signs
- Natural resources
- Weather
- Landmarks

Color is used on all types of maps to show
different kinds of information. Color is used on
• political maps to show the areas of different
  countries or states,
• physical maps to show the different textures of
  the earth's surface, and on
• special purpose maps to show information such
  as quantities.

Where to Find Maps

There are many different places where you can find a variety of maps. Here are just a few:

- The library (look in the card catalog under the name of the place)
- Travel agencies
- Automobile clubs
- Gas stations

There are also many different resources that contain maps such as:

- Atlases
- Encyclopedias
- Books about travel
- Magazines
- Newspapers

Using an Atlas

An atlas is a collection of maps that are bound together to form a book. Many atlases include:

- Information about how to use an atlas and general facts about maps
- Photographs, drawings, tables, and graphs
- Articles that give facts about such things as climate, population, and history
- A glossary of terms

There are many different atlases available. When you are looking for an atlas, keep these things in mind:

- Look at the date of publication. You want to make sure the atlas is up-to-date.
- Look to see what types of maps are included.
- Look at the introductory material. Make sure the instructions for using the atlas are clear and easy to follow.

Using a Gazetteer

A gazetteer is a dictionary of geography that lists places around the world. Instead of using maps, the gazetteer gives brief descriptions about each place. The information usually includes:

- The location of the place
- The correct pronunciation of the place's name
- What the place is, such as a town, country, or river
- A brief description
- Historical information

Making a Map

Now that you know how to read a map, you can try making your own. If you start out by making a simple map, you will see how easy and fun it can be. You will need to follow three simple steps, and you will need

- unlined paper,
- a lead pencil with an eraser,
- a ruler, and
- colored pencils or pens.

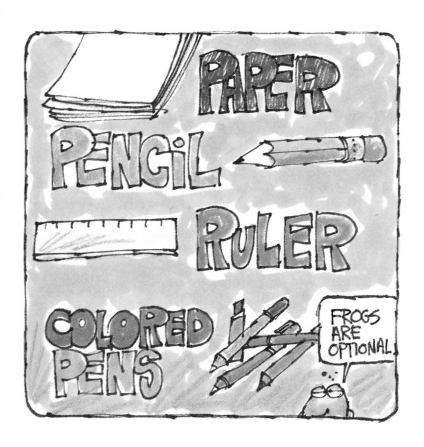

Step One: Decide on the purpose of your map.
Before you begin drawing your map, you need to answer some important questions.

- What information do you want your map to show?
- What area do you want to include in your map?
- What type of map will best display the information?

Step Two: Draw the basic outline of your map.
Now it is time to begin drawing your map. To start, use a lead pencil with an eraser so you can make changes and corrections as you work.

- Decide on the scale you will use and write it down in the bottom corner of your map.
- Determine the direction of your map and draw a symbol that shows which way your map will face.
- Draw the area that is included in your map.

Step Three: Complete your map.
The final step is to plot the information on your map. Record the information in lead pencil and then color the map with your colored pencils or pens.

- Decide how to display the information. Decide if you want to use picture symbols or just colors. Plot the information on your map.
- Make a legend or key and draw in the symbols and their explanations.
- Make an index if necessary.

2" = 1 block

□ = Big Screen TV.

▽ = Great Snacks

ᗧ = Video Games

☠ = Makes you Work

🍦 = Good place to play

☺ = Swimming pool

WARNING!

If you follow the suggestions in this book...

...you will discover a whole new world!

THE END

About the Author

Marilyn Berry has a master's degree in education with a specialization in reading. She is on staff as a creator of supplementary materials at Living Skills Press. Marilyn and her husband Steve Patterson have two sons, John and Brent.